ST. JOSEPH, MY REAL ESTATE AGENT

St. Joseph, My Real Estate Agent

Patron Saint of Home Life and Home Selling

STEPHEN J. BINZ

Note to readers: The term "Realtor" designates a registered collective membership mark that identifies a real estate professional who is a member of the National Association of Realtors.

The Scripture quotations contained herein are from the *New Revised Standard Version Bible*, copyright ©1989 by the Division of Christian Education of the National Council of the Churches of Christ in the USA. Used by permission. All rights reserved.

Cover design: Candle Light Studios

LIBRARY OF CONGRESS CATALOGING-IN-PUBLICATION DATA
Binz, Stephen J., 1955-
  St. Joseph, my real estate agent : patron saint of home life and home-selling / Stephen J. Binz.
     p. cm.
  ISBN 1-56955-361-0 (alk. paper)
  1. Joseph, Saint. I. Title.
  BS2458.B56 2003
  232.9'32–dc21

                                                              2003001789

ISBN 978-1-56955-361-9

Published by Servant Books, an imprint of
Franciscan Media
28 W. Liberty St.
Cincinnati, OH 45202
www.FranciscanMedia.org

Printed in the United States of America.

Printed on acid-free paper.

14 15 16 17   15 14 13 12 11 10 9

*C*ontents

Foreword

$\mathcal{M}$ ost people buy and sell a home at least once in their lives. Many people buy and sell frequently. Yet, the experience is always fraught with emotion and often marked by anxiety. Buying and selling houses usually happens at transitional moments in people's lives: a marriage, a birth, a divorce, a job transfer, an illness, or a death. These are times in which people often feel insecure and need some of life's intangibles like friendship, support, prayer, and divine assistance.

My home-selling experience happened at one of those transitional periods of life, the end of a relationship and the beginning of an uncertain future. It was a time of both sadness and hope, a time when I needed assistance and encouragement. As the opening chapter of this book describes, that support came in an unusual form and in an unexpected way.

My discovery of St. Joseph changed my life. Though I have always been a person of rather traditional Christian faith, I never knew that life is

7

made up of little miracles. Though I've always believed in a heavenly life for those who have died, I never really experienced the fact that they could share that life with me. Though I always knew that I could pray to God and that he answers prayers, I never realized that my everyday life could be concretely blessed with God's abundance.

I have come to appreciate that life offers us daily reminders of grace, of God's loving presence among us. And if we learn to look for it, we can experience grace in surprising and heartwarming ways. Some people call these surprises miracles. Perhaps they are. These frequent, even daily, occurrences that seem out of the ordinary come unexpectedly and remind us that our lives are not in our hands. These little events help us learn to trust in a higher and loving power that is greater than our temporal pursuits.

In addition to being grateful to St. Joseph, I am thankful to some special people who led me to him. I want to acknowledge Janet and Bud Jones of the Janet Jones Company in Little Rock. Their professional staff of Realtors makes home buying and selling a pleasurable adventure for their clients. I am grateful to Susan Reynolds, my Realtor and friend, and to Donna Dailey, who sold my home "to Joseph." I am also inspired by all the Realtors I have come to know McKay and Company, Rainey Realty, Rector-Phillips-Morse, Charlotte John Company, Roddy McCaskill Realty, Adkins McNeill Smith & Associates, Coldwell Banker, ReMax, ERA, Century 21 and others.

My friend Louise Perrotta of St. Paul, Minnesota, has written the best book on St. Joseph in print today, *Saint Joseph: His Life and His Role in the Church Today.* From discussions with her and from her writings, I grew to understand the role that St. Joseph can play in my life. I thank Susan Pitman, my former associate in magazine publishing, whose insights and care made the intercession of St. Joseph real for me. I am truly grateful for several people who read this manuscript and offered helpful suggestions, especially Deb Halter, Angie Peters, Amy Bradford, and Cynthia Cavnar. I am indebted to Bert Ghezzi, editorial director for Servant Publications, who saw the potential in my work and encouraged me to publish. And to my mom and dad; brother and sisters, Sharon, Sandy, and Mike;

nieces and nephews, Melony, Cristin, Brent, Nikki, Jennifer, Heather, Kyle, and Kody: thank you for teaching me the joys of life at home.

I would like this work to honor my grandfather, Joseph Binz. During his earthly life, which began in 1897 and spanned the entire twentieth century, he honored St. Joseph by imitating his qualities. He was a craftsman with exquisite skills, a man of trusting faith in God, a loving husband, and an outstanding father. Unlike ancient Joseph, my grandfather lived to see his children's children's children; he was a great-grandfather.

Above all, I want to acknowledge that the only purpose of devotion to the saints, like the purpose of our own lives as well, is to give greater glory to God. Together with all the instruments of God's love, both on earth and in heaven, I pray that all glory and praise be given to God alone, from whom all blessings flow.

1

$\mathcal{H}$ouse-Selling:
Joseph the Realtor

$\mathcal{S}$usan, my real estate agent, was an optimistic, thirty-something Presbyterian, extremely competent and determined. I contacted her about selling my home and she made all the necessary arrangements for putting the property on the market. This house, we decided, would sell quickly because of its location, and I had already begun to look for a new home.

Once the "For Sale" sign was up, I kept the place squeaky clean and turned on all the lights and raised all the shades as one couple or family after another came to see the house. The first Sunday open house attracted more than thirty people who commented favorably on the nice home they could make their own. But a month went by with several near misses. There had been some genuine interest, but no offers yet.

"Steve, have you considered burying a statue of St. Joseph?" Susan asked me one day.

"Have I what?" I said incredulously.

"You've heard of that practice, haven't you?" she said. "People bury a statue of St. Joseph in their yard, and then their house sells. Surely you've heard of people doing that. It works nearly every time," she added, matter-of-factly.

I was shocked at my professional Realtor. I knew her pretty well by now and had begun to admire her confidence, her faith, and her trusting attitude about life. I had followed all of her advice up to the present to prepare my home for a sale. But this threw me for a loop: Bury a statue in my yard in order to lure a buyer?!

"Susan, that is the most ridiculous, most superstitious thing I've ever heard," I said finally. "I am not going to bury a plastic statue in the yard in order to get what I want from God. I can't think of anything more crude and illogical. Let's think of other ways we can sell this house."

Well ... six more months passed. I had already bought a new home with a bridge loan and was beginning to pay double mortgages. My previous home had generated lots of interest on the market, but it hadn't drawn a single offer. Feeling panicked and getting desperate, I called my Realtor.

"Susan," I said sheepishly, "tell me more about this St. Joseph thing you mentioned a few months ago."

She good-naturedly told me about the custom. People who want to sell their home bury a statue of St. Joseph upside down in their yard as a sign they are asking for his help. Usually after the burial amazing things begin to happen and the house often sells within a short time. After the sale, the sellers unearth the statue and honor the image of Joseph in their new home.

Susan told me that she knew hundreds of people who had buried a statue with good results. "But don't feel like you need to do it," she said. "Obviously you're not comfortable with doing something like that. Don't worry about it; it was just an idea."

But I started to think that maybe I should investigate this matter further. As a writer, I try to find out everything I can about a subject from as many angles as possible. I remembered that one of my writer friends had just finished a book on St. Joseph. So I e-mailed Louise: "You know a lot about St. Joseph. Tell me about this practice of burying his statue to sell a house." Louise wrote back that most of the time the ritual tends to be a rather superstitious practice, one that she didn't put much stock in. But, she added, if I did it in faith, she thought it could be a genuinely prayerful experience.

"Do it in faith." Well, I do believe in the saints, I reasoned. I know that I can ask the saints to pray for me just as I ask my friends on earth to pray for me. I truly believe that God answers prayers. But wasn't this a bit too self-serving a request for one of God's saints? Yes, I believe in prayer and the intercession of the saints. But burying a statue in the ground? I guessed that would hold Joseph captive until he gave in to my request. How quaint and primitive!

One of my work associates was a Catholic whom I respected for her convictions and wisdom. Maybe she would have some thoughts on the matter. "Oh sure," she said when I asked her about it. "St. Joseph will definitely help you with this. Oh, the burying in the ground part? Well, you know how we Catholics are," she said. "We always use the things of this world to touch the divine—water, bread, wine, oil, pictures, statues, fire, dirt, whatever. It's all part of the prayer. We are sensual beings. We need to touch something real to get us in touch with God. Getting down on your knees and digging in the dirt is part of the ritual. It's a humbling experience, and it gets you close to God's earth."

Hmm... This still sounded strange, but I thought it demonstrated a kind of intuitive, irrational logic. I guess I could make this a genuine experience of prayer. If I were going to do it, though, I would need to do it right, if for no other reason than my spiritual integrity.

So, I thought, my first step would be to find a statue. I didn't want a cheap, plastic statue. To follow through with this and honor the image of Joseph in my new home, I needed a noble statue. So I purchased an alabaster statue from a religious goods dealer. It was nice. I liked it. Joseph looked fairly human, with a knowing smile on his face and the saw and carpenter's tools in his hands.

Since the secret of making this experience meaningful was to approach it as a prayer and not a superstitious act, I decided to set a day and a time to perform this ritual and to invite my friends to pray with me. I chose Thursday at noon, a time when I knew I could get home and when most people pause in their day. Admittedly, noon was also when I knew that most of my neighbors would be at work, and I wouldn't have to worry about their suspicious eyes.

I e-mailed lots of my friends, called my family members, spoke to several church friends, and of course invited Susan, my Realtor, to pray with me.

Here's my e-mail message:

"Dear Friends, I am going to do something that I have resisted doing for awhile. I am preparing to bury a statue of St. Joseph in my yard and pray for the sale of my home. As you know, I've had it up for sale for seven months without a bite, and now it's time to seek some celestial help. Some trusted friends have told

me that St. Joseph would help me in this matter, so I'm going to ask for his intercession.

On Thursday at noon I'm going to bury a
statue of St. Joseph in my yard and ask that
God's will be done with my house—and done
quickly. I'm asking that you pause at noon on
Thursday and lift up a prayer with me. Pray
that my home sells soon and that the family
who buys my house will make a peaceful
home here. Thank you. Steve."

As I hit "SEND," a strange sense of excitement
and anticipation washed over me. Soon, I started
receiving e-mail responses from friends across the
country assuring me of their prayers. "Don't forget
to bury him upside down and facing the street,"
wrote my friend Bob, from Milwaukee. I knew that
he was joking, but also serious; he was having fun
with me but was also confident of the value of popular rituals.

As all these events transpired, the saint, the man from ancient Nazareth, slowly started becoming real to me. I began to think about how he had found a home for Mary and Jesus, and how he must have worried often about their financial condition and whether he could meet his family's needs. I thought about my grandfather, also named Joseph. He had died a couple of years before, at age 101, after a life of hard work and deep faith. He had provided a secure home for my grandmother, my father, and my aunt and uncle. My father and I had been given the name Joseph as our middle names, in honor of my grandfather, and ultimately in honor of St. Joseph, husband of Mary and foster father of Jesus.

This saint of heaven was beginning to feel like part of my family. *Maybe he really cares about me*, I thought, *just as my grandfather cared about me as I was growing up. Maybe St. Joseph truly wants to look after my welfare from his place in heaven. Maybe he wants to teach me some of the things he learned during his earthly sojourn two thousand years ago—things like trust, and the value of prayer, and the importance of staying close to family and friends.*

Heaven was starting to seem much closer. Joseph was no longer just a figure from the distant past, a character from biblical history. He had become a real man, enjoying the fullness of life with God but able to care about me. This saint of heaven, I discovered, keeps in close touch with the earth.

So Thursday came, and soon it was noon. I knelt in my front yard in front of the hole I had dug. My dirt-covered hands clutched the statue of venerable Joseph. I can't remember feeling more uplifted, more confident, more in touch with God than I felt at that moment. This skeptic had turned believer. I offered up a silent prayer and felt the prayerful support of lots of people. I knew that my new friend Joseph would help me with my struggles and wouldn't let me down.

Placing the statue upside down in the ground, still confused about the upside-down part of the rite, I turned the dirt back over it. The deed was done. Not too many people had driven by with wondering eyes. I didn't think that the neighbors had seen my primitive ritual. I had no need to explain to incredulous onlookers, and I would tell only those I wished to know about my zealous deed. I knew that something would happen soon, but I didn't know what it would be.

Later that day, my Realtor called to say a potential buyer would be coming by. The next day, three people looked at the house. Five days later, one man decided to come for a second look. My Realtor told me that he was serious and sure enough, on the seventh day after I buried the statue, he made an offer to buy my house.

When I went to Susan's office to look over the offer, I noticed the signature on the paperwork: The buyer's name was Joseph. Of course, it would be, I thought. The next day I made a counteroffer, and on the ninth day the deal closed. I sold the house to Joseph.

Maybe the house would have sold without my burying the statue. Maybe it had been destined to sell a week later anyway. Maybe the real gift of St. Joseph had been to help me trust, reconnect me with some old friends, and experience the closeness of God in a new way. Maybe Joseph had given me the gift of knowing that my faith was real, intertwined with my daily life and concrete needs. Whatever it was, the gift was abundant. I felt grateful and blessed.

After I sold my house, I began to wonder again about the details of the ritual of burying a statue. I could understand the value of having a visual image of the saint. I could even understand the significance of digging in the dirt on my knees. But why upside down? Wasn't that just a little absurd? "Joseph," I asked, "what about this burying upside down?"

Here's the friendly answer I received from him: "You've had a lot of fun doing this and I appreciate the lighthearted, childlike, trusting way that you've gone about this prayerful ritual. A sense of humor is so important in human relationships. You know, I have a sense of humor, too. And I'd really enjoy it if you would use your sense of humor in relationship to me, just as you do with your other friends." *Okay,* I thought. *I can do that.*

2

Real Estate in Nazareth

There is good reason why my new heavenly friend, Joseph, is the patron saint of homes. He provided a home for the most outstanding family who ever lived. But his life has been so overshadowed by the lives of Jesus and Mary, many of us hardly think about him. Yet, it is in large part due to Joseph that Jesus was able to grow in wisdom and experience.

I began to research and reflect on the historical life of Joseph. My sources were the Bible, which provides limited information about Joseph, and modern research into life at the time of Jesus. I knew that my newly discovered devotion to St. Joseph would continue to flourish as I explored his real, earthly life.

By all outward appearances, Joseph of Nazareth could not have been a more ordinary person. He did not live in any of the great cities of the world. He did not inherit any worldly position that would allow him to rise to fame. He made his home in a very out-of-the-way place in circumstances that were anything but privileged. In the ancient world, important people were supposed to come from important places. But the expected ways are rarely God's ways, a lesson that Joseph was teaching me abundantly.

Real estate in Nazareth was not considered a good investment during the Roman era when Joseph lived. No one wanted to move to Nazareth from Jerusalem, Caesarea, Tiberius, or any of the large cities of ancient Palestine. This small village in lower Galilee was off the beaten path. It was not on any of the major Roman roads, and it was quite a distance from the commercially viable fishing villages around the Sea of Galilee. In fact, there was little to tempt prospective buyers to the remote village of Nazareth. The town had a population of only a few hundred, and most of the young people there yearned to leave for the larger cities with more abundant opportunities.

Historical research and archaeology offer us a great deal of information about the age in which Joseph lived. Based on what we know about the architecture and lifestyle of Joseph's day, we can paint a fairly accurate picture of his home. The house that Joseph chose for his family, primitive by all modern standards, probably consisted of three or four rooms joined to an open courtyard shared by several other houses. The walls were made of fieldstones, held together with smaller stones packed into the crevices, and smeared with a plaster made of mud, straw, and chaff for insulation.

The floors were of beaten earth or clay.

The rooms were used for preparing food, eating meals, sleeping, and storing the necessities of life. The living room contained the hearth for winter warmth, light, and cooking. In one corner of the room sat the frame and loom, used for spinning and weaving threads into cloth. Pegs, hooks, and niches around the walls provided off-the-floor storage.

Like many houses built along hillsides, the home of Joseph was probably built around a natural cave which served as part of the living space. These domestic caves were the only heating and cooling system available, staying warm and dry in the winter and pleasantly cool in the summer.

With only one entrance, the house featured a hewn threshold with a stone doorjamb and a wooden door. A few windows high in the walls were designed for ventilation and lighting rather than scenic views. Doorways to the rooms inside the house were framed with simple wood beams and covered with curtains.

Joseph's house included an extra room for his carpentry workshop where he could work on rainy days and store his tools. Excavations in Nazareth indicate that its inhabitants took advantage of the soft limestone to dig basements, cisterns, and storage bins underneath the ground level of their homes. Storage rooms in Joseph's house would have contained supplies of grain and milled flour for cooking, feed for animals, and chaff for plastering and brick-making. Storage baskets near the kitchen held cheeses, dried fruits, and produce, and jugs held supplies of olive oil and wine.

Space was at a premium. Children would never fight to have their own rooms. People lived close to one another and the modern need for "personal space" was unheard of. Clay lamps fueled with olive oil lit the dark rooms. The family ate meals while sitting cross-legged on the floor at a low table.

Joseph, Mary, and their family would have shared their home with the family animals, especially the goats, which were family pets and sources for dairy products.

The roof of the house served as an important place for domestic activity. The people of Nazareth would often go up to the roof to pray, visit with guests, dry their clothes, or take an afternoon siesta. They accessed the flat area by climbing an inside ladder or the outside stairs. The roof was made by fixing poles or slats perpendicular to the ceiling beams and covering them with plaster made of chaff and mud. They needed to be replastered each year before the rainy season to seal cracks which developed during the summer heat.

Much of the day-to-day life of Nazareth took place outdoors because the weather was generally mild throughout the year, and indoors was dark and cramped. During most of the year, the skies were cloudless and the temperature ranged between 45 and 85 degrees Fahrenheit. During the rainy winter season, the rains came intermittently, followed by several days of dry weather. But the rains were always welcome, as villagers collected rainwater in the cisterns and saved it for the dry periods.

The courtyard, which set the scene for most of family life, translates into our modern-day living room, workshop, garage, and dining room, all in one. A fence wrapped a portion of the area for goat pens, and chickens roamed the enclosure freely. Several families shared the outdoor oven and the grinding stone nearby. The oven, made of clay bricks, sat in a corner of the courtyard. The aroma of baked bread and cooking spices filled the air throughout the day. In the courtyard and in the streets, children played games. Women drew water from the one spring in the village and carried it to their homes in clay jars balanced on their heads.

An abundance of olive trees, which grew easily

on the rocky hillsides, surrounded the village. Joseph often used the wood of the olive tree, with its beautiful grain, for his carpentry. The village olive press extracted the olive oil, so essential for lamp fuel, cooking, and ointments. Vines with deep purple grapes spread over the slopes of the hill. The villagers seasonally cut back the vines with pruning hooks, then harvested the grapes and trampled the fruits in the grape presses to make syrup, vinegar, and wine.

Various grains, including barley, wheat, and millet, grew in the fields around Nazareth. Farmers brought the harvested grain to the threshing floor at the edge of the village and spread it out to dry. There they separated the seed kernels from the husks by means of a threshing sledge dragged repeatedly across the grain by an ox or donkey. When the wind was blowing, the farmers would throw the grain into the air with a winnowing fork, using the wind to separate the seed, straw, and chaff according to weight.

Terraces built along the slopes maximized the harvests as they were irrigated from the one spring trickling through the village. The people of Nazareth cultivated fig and pomegranate trees as well as gardens with legumes and vegetables. The residents of this out-of-the-way hamlet worked toward one goal: self-sufficiency. If they could grow all they needed, pay their taxes, and not make trouble for the Roman authorities, they could live a pleasant life.

So, a home in Nazareth seldom showed up as a featured property in the real estate scroll of the *Galilee Times*. Rarely would a Realtor have flagged a Nazareth property with a "Don't miss this one" ad. When a home went up for sale in Nazareth, an agent would have to honestly state something like this: "Four-room fixer-upper built in the cliffs of Nazareth. Exterior, stone and mud plaster; interior, stone and mud plaster. Pleasant temperature control due to interior cave. Underground basement for storage. Roof replaced last dry season. Spacious courtyard shared with four other homes. Workshop and garden plots included. Occupants eager to sell. Moving to the city."

Usually one's hometown has at least one claim to fame—it was the site of an important historical event, for example, or the home of a famous person. But not Nazareth. Neither the Jewish Scriptures nor any of the writings of ancient Jewish historians made a single reference to Nazareth. People from the cities knew little about the town; it was the kind of place that city folk ridiculed. The derogatory comment made by Nathaniel in the Gospel of John, "Can anything good come from Nazareth?" (John 1:46), probably typified the response of outsiders.

Scholars don't know how Joseph came to make his home in this village. According to the genealogies from the gospels, his family was from Judea in the south, from the town of Bethlehem, the hometown of his ancestor King David. It seems logical that this descendant of David would be living in Judea, around Bethlehem. But with all the wars and exiles of the Jewish people through the centuries, the people of the original tribes had been dislocated from their original tribal homelands and sent into foreign lands. When they eventually returned, they settled in other areas of Israel.

Many have speculated that a clan of Davidic descendants must have settled in Galilee in the years before the coming of Jesus and named their town Nazareth. The name comes from a Hebrew word which literally means "branch," an image of the awaited Messiah that came from the prophets. Isaiah the prophet had proclaimed that a "Branch" from the root of Jesse, the father of David, would bear fruit (see Isaiah 11:1). This village of the Branch, then, was where Joseph made his home and brought the young Jesus after his family's exile in Egypt.

This small clan of Nazarenes knew that the prophets had said some amazing things about the destiny of their family. The tree of David had been cut down long before, but the stump of Jesse contained the potential for new growth. The root of David's line was still alive in Joseph's heritage. Yet the people of Nazareth could not imagine much of anything happening after generations of upheaval and dislocation. Now they lived in an out-of-the-way place, far from their ancestral Bethlehem and from the holy city Jerusalem. Though they lived with some distant sense of expectation, they did not anticipate much happening in the hills of Galilee.

Yet, because Joseph lived in this tiny hamlet, Jesus came to be known as the Nazorean, the man from the village of the Branch. When the Gospel of Matthew narrates that Joseph brought Jesus to live in this place, after exile in Egypt, it indicates that the words of the prophets were fulfilled (see Matthew 2:23). He is that righteous Branch, growing from the roots of Jesse and David, that will blossom and bear fruit for the world.

Despite the fact that Nazareth was an unknown backwater, it did have one very special quality. The town was set on a mountainous ridge, about 1,650 feet above sea level at its highest point. An afternoon stroll to the south of the town would offer a panoramic view of the valley below. But this was no ordinary valley, it was the Jezreel Valley. Few places are more significant for the long history of Israel than this vast plain below hilly Nazareth.

The Jezreel Valley formed part of the ancient Via Maris, the Way of the Sea, connecting Egypt in the southwest with Damascus in the northeast. It had been the area's most important trade route since ancient times. For centuries, caravans of traders and mighty armies had passed through this valley. Joseph must have come here often to watch the travelers pass by far below. He probably tried to imagine their destinations and visualize life in those distant and exotic places. Maybe he imagined that his children would eventually leave Nazareth and have an opportunity to make an impact in the larger world. Perhaps this view is the reason Joseph chose to make his home in Nazareth.

There was no way that Joseph could have imagined the global impact his simple life would have. Seldom are we privileged to understand the full significance of our daily words and actions in the lives of others. But the line of Joseph did indeed blossom and bear fruit for the world. The little town of Nazareth became one of the most notable and visited cities of the earth. For two thousand years, people from throughout the world have come to this place because the life of Joseph's son made the ground holy. People journey here by the millions for enrichment, inspiration, and transformation because the "son of the carpenter" called this place home.

The Nazareth of today is a good-sized city that is

bustling, noisy, and crowded. It thrives on tourists and pilgrims who come there to touch the places holding memories of Jesus, Mary, and Joseph, who lived most of their lives there. Palestinian Christians and Muslims populate the city, and Jews who immigrated from many parts of the world inhabit a newer settlement above the ancient city, called Nazareth Illit. The sights and sounds of the city are typical of the Holy Land: prayers chanted from the mosques, bells tolling from the churches, Arab men with heads wrapped in kefiyas, Jewish men with skullcaps, women in head scarves, and Franciscans in brown habits.

Twenty centuries separate today's Nazareth from the town inhabited by history's most famous family. Layer upon layer of occupational remains stacked atop the ancient town provide evidence of past eras. Beneath the cars and buses, houses and hotels of today lies the Jewish peasant village. From the fifth century on, there have been two significant churches in Nazareth. One church honors the house of Joseph where Jesus was raised, the other honors the house of Mary, where she received the message of an angel that she was to be the mother of God's Son. Today the Church of St. Joseph and the nearby Basilica of the Annunciation mark those places where God called the ordinary family of Nazareth to do extraordinary things.

In modern Nazareth we can still observe many characteristics of an ancient oriental town. The souk, or marketplace, displays fruits and vegetables, live chickens and fresh meat, woven cloths and jewelry. In the shop owners and craftsmen of the town we can still see people like Joseph, with his olive skin and deep-set eyes. A sixth-century pilgrim said that the women of Nazareth were more beautiful than the other women of the country, a characteristic attributed to Mary, whom the women claim as their relative. In the children who play in the streets and carry their books to school, we can imagine the young Jesus who called this town his home.

Clearly, real estate in Nazareth has changed in the past two millennia in features, in attraction, and in value. As I look at the statue of St. Joseph that now sits on the mantel in my living room, I wonder about the impact of my home on the lives of the people who fill my life. Since we live our lives forward, but understand them backward, we cannot know the future value of what we do each day. But like Joseph, I know that my home is a simple gift where my heart gets renewed and restored as I try to do my best in the life I have been given.

3

Home-Making in Nazareth

We can describe our houses in objective language: square feet, style, color, and décor. But the language we use to describe "home" must somehow combine the physical structures in which we live with all the activities, emotions, memories, and hopes associated with that place. I've enjoyed painting the walls of my new house and expressing my eclectic tastes with furnishings. But when I hang my pictures and have my family and friends for dinner, I'll begin to experience home within these walls.

"Home is where the heart is," the ancient proverb

proclaims. Joseph wanted his new wife, Mary, to learn to feel this way about the house to which he would move her. But it would take a long time of enduring challenging experiences, bearing sorrows, and celebrating joys before the house in Nazareth would become the home of Joseph and Mary. The bond of committed love transforms a spot on the map into a place in the heart.

The life cycle in ancient Nazareth was far more condensed than our twenty-first-century experience. Today, people marry and have children at increasingly later ages; the life expectancy rises every year; and living for a century no longer makes headlines. Joseph's life expectancy was about forty years. Girls married at about age fourteen, and most people died in their thirties or forties after raising a large family. An infection or flu virus could easily be a death knell. Famine was never further away than a drought or bad harvest. Life was lived perilously close to the edge.

Joseph had little land and no cash, and probably just barely eked out a living and paid his taxes. His body, we can imagine, bore the scars of hard work. Trade was impractical, requiring a slow, hungry ox and a cart to transport goods over barely existing roads. The concept of upward mobility was unknown, and social movement was mostly downward, as several sons would divide their father's land, providing increasingly less land for every new generation.

People stayed home a lot in the hillside hamlets of Galilee. There were no public theaters, no bath-houses, no agora or shopping district, no paved streets lined with columns for cosmopolitan strolls—all of which were enjoyed by people living in large cities. The streets of Nazareth were narrow and crooked, and when the sun set the village got very dark.

Much of home life revolved around family meals. The healthy Mediterranean diet, so touted today, was the daily fare in Nazareth: grains, olives, and grapes. Meals were served in clay pots, casserole dishes, and bowls. They often consisted of a stew with lentils and seasonal vegetables ladled on pita bread, sometimes with cheese, yogurt, nuts, and fruit on the side. A cup of local wine took the edge off a hard day's work.

This is the type of home life in which Jesus was raised. Here he learned to walk and talk, and eventually to read. His first words were probably *abba* and *imma*, Aramaic for "dada" and "mama." The songs that Mary and Joseph sang at home were the psalms of Israel and the folk tunes of their people. They nurtured a strong awareness of the presence of God in their home.

The family was the bearer of the religious tradition, so all the earliest religious educational experiences of Jesus occurred in his home. The first prayers Jesus ever heard were voiced by his parents. Jesus learned to honor God not only through the words of his parents, but also through their activities: lighting the lamps, making the foods and symbols of Israel's feasts, and offering silent and vocal prayers of praise and intercession. At home in Nazareth, Jesus began to sense the goodness and the awesomeness of God.

Joseph instructed Jesus in the traditional method of Jewish religious education just as he had learned from his father. He taught Jesus from his earliest years to recognize God as the Creator of the world and the Redeemer of his people, as the one who had guided Israel out of slavery to a life of freedom in their own land.

Both at home and at the synagogue, Jesus learned the ancient Hebrew language of his people and studied the sacred traditions of Israel. He read the Torah and the Prophets and chanted the psalms, so that by the age of thirteen, he was ready to become a full member of the people of Israel, a bar mitzvah or "son of the commandment."

Twice a day, morning and evening, the family

recited the "Shema" from the book of Deuteronomy: "Hear, O Israel: The Lord is our God, the
Lord alone. You shall love the Lord your God with
all your heart, and with all your soul, and with all
your might. Keep these words that I am command-
ing you today in your heart. Recite them to your
children and talk about them when you are at
home and when you are away, when you lie down
and when you rise" (Deuteronomy 6:4-7). This pas-
sage served as the core of faith for Joseph, Mary,
and Jesus. They knew that God was one, that above
all life was about loving God, and that this faith was
to be the center of discussion and reflection
throughout their days.

Joseph had carved a tiny wooden box to cover
and protect a strip of parchment inscribed with the
words of the Shema. He nailed this mezuza to his
doorpost, as was the custom in most Jewish homes.
Every day, when leaving home and returning, Joseph
would touch the box containing the scroll and in

devotion kiss his fingers, reminding himself of his life's center. Daily home rituals such as this imbued the heart of Jesus with the faith of his ancestors. As an adult, Jesus would teach this home prayer, the Shema, as the greatest of all God's commandments (see Mark 12:29-30).

Toward sunset on Friday evenings, the tenor of the town changed. Everyone in Nazareth came in from six days of work in order to end the week with the Sabbath, the holy day of rest. Before the sunset, Mary had prepared the Sabbath meal, and as the sun sank below the horizon, she lit the Sabbath lamps and Joseph recited the Sabbath prayers: "Blessed are you, Lord, God of all creation...." Joseph blessed the cup of wine and the fresh loaves of bread, and he blessed his family and gave thanks to God. The Sabbath dusk brought a joyful spirit and the evening continued with singing, dining, and lively dancing.

On the Sabbath, from sundown Friday to sundown

Saturday, the villagers were prohibited from working, traveling, buying, or selling. These were Jewish
laws set up to safeguard the Sabbath as a day of joy
and peace. The people of Nazareth often spent the
morning of the Sabbath learning Scripture in the
synagogue and the afternoons socializing in
leisure. The holy day elevated the rather routine
life of every day and reminded the Jewish people of
God's blessings.

On the Sabbath, at daily meals and seasonal feasts,
at birth and death and through all the stages of life,
the families of Nazareth passed on their traditions.
Some of the most important parts of a religious
education in the home spring from the questions
that children ask. All children like to ask questions,
and clever parents do things that provoke good
questions. One of these questions has been ritual-
ized in the annual Passover meal. During the meal,
the youngest child of the family asks, "Why is this
night different from all other nights?" Thus begins

the recounting of the story of Exodus. But all the questions of children become teaching opportunities for parents to explain the traditions of their people and to instill a reverence for God within their hearts.

The spiritual nurturing of children is one of the greatest gifts of home life. Faith is not just taught, it is caught. Every Jewish child in ancient Nazareth knew about Moses and the Exodus because of the Feast of Passover, about Esther because of the festival of Purim, about Judas Maccabeus because of Hanukkah. These were their stories and their stories made them who they were. Feasts, rituals, and celebration made Joseph's house a home to remember.

From his heavenly home, Joseph still remembers what it is like to create a home. He understands the teaching power of customs and traditions for raising a family. He knows that prayer and rituals bond a family in love. He understands that rest and celebration are as important as work and daily responsibility. He knows that life is short and that instilling memories is a great gift as life goes on.

Joseph, a tender spouse and a wise parent, knew that home is where the heart is. As I try to create a home for those I love, I can look to Joseph to help me. I can try to imitate his example and absorb his wisdom.

4

*A*way From Home:
Traveler, Refugee, and Pilgrim

*D*espite the fact that people generally didn't travel much in rural Galilee, most of the information we have about Joseph from the Christian Bible shows him on the road away from home. He traveled with Mary to Bethlehem, where Jesus was born; he traveled to Egypt in order to protect his new child; and he traveled often to Jerusalem for the feasts and rituals of his Jewish faith. Joseph spent several of his best years as a husband

and father longing to return home. Because there is no place like home, perhaps like most of us, Joseph carried his home with him in his heart.

For me, home is my base. Sometimes I find it in the structures of my house and sometimes in the memories and longings of my heart. I've lived in many places, so several houses in which I've lived seem like home to me. I enjoy adventurous journeys, but I find the best part about travel is coming back home, making the souvenirs part of my décor, and looking at the photos while securely huddled in front of the fireplace. I keep my traveling memories with me and integrate them into my heart's home.

Traveler

The gospel narrative of Jesus' birth brings us from a domestic setting in Nazareth into a journey of worldwide proportions. The emperor in far-away Rome had called for a census that would involve the whole earth. So a decree issued in Rome set the world on a journey. The birth of Jesus became part of this universal event, a foreshadowing of the global impact that this newborn child would later create.

Caesar Augustus, the ruler of the world, was considered semi-divine. The royal insignia of the period proclaimed him "savior of the whole world," and he was most recognized for the era of peace that he established during his reign. Augustus' decree brought Joseph from his tiny hamlet in Galilee to the town of Bethlehem, where his child would be born. No one—not even Joseph—could imagine at the time that this child would be the true Savior, the one who would bring real peace to the earth.

Ironically, the journey made by the people of the world would not be to exotic places, but back to their own hometowns. It really would be a journey home, to the place of their ancestors. So Joseph went from his own home in Nazareth to the home of his forefathers in Bethlehem.

Many people in modern times research their

family history and visit the hometown of their ancestors. They experience a deep sense of nostalgia and rootedness as they return to the homes of their grandparents, great-grandparents, and even more far-removed members of their family tree. People look up distant relatives in the phone book of their hometown; search cemeteries for the names of relatives from the past; look up birth documents and records; and even try to find the neighborhood or house where they lived.

Returning to Bethlehem provided this kind of nostalgic experience for Joseph, who had probably traveled to Bethlehem often to visit relatives. His most famous ancestor had been King David, Israel's most beloved ruler. Bethlehem, the town of King David's origin, was where young David had taken care of the flock of his father, Jesse. It was the town to which the prophet had come and anointed Jesse's youngest son, making him the future king. Because Joseph was of the lineage of David, his family belonged to the royal house of David, the line from which Israel expected its Messiah.

Bethlehem speaks of great things coming from small and humble beginnings. From here, the shepherd boy became the king. Here, the infant son of Mary and Joseph was born, the one the whole world had been awaiting. His first visitors were simple shepherds caring for their flocks in the fields. To them, the angel announced that the newborn child was the Savior, Messiah, and Lord. When they went to see this child, they found him in a manger, a feeding trough for animals. The hope of the world slept in a manger full of straw. Bethlehem, the ancestral home of Joseph, would forever be remembered as the birthplace of Jesus, his first home on earth.

Refugee

After the birth of Jesus, Joseph and his family set out on another journey. This time they became refugees, people forced to flee from their home to protect their lives. King Herod, notorious for his cruelty and paranoia, felt threatened by the widespread expectation among the Jews of a coming messianic king. So when he received news from the Magi that a child had been born who was destined to be king, he responded with fear and rage. He ordered the massacre of all the boys age two and under in Bethlehem and its vicinity. The families with new sons suddenly felt their joy turn to bitter grief.

But Jesus was not among King Herod's victims. God had revealed to Joseph in a dream that the king wanted to kill Jesus. An angel told Joseph to take Jesus and Mary to Egypt to flee from Herod's wrath. Joseph rose in the night, gathered some meager supplies, and, under cover of night, escaped with his family. Whether they made the two-hundred-mile journey from Bethlehem to the area of modern-day Cairo alone, or eventually joined a caravan of travelers, the trek was surely filled with hardship and fear. Like refugees in all eras of history, Joseph's life became precarious in a way it had never been before. Constantly looking over his shoulder, Joseph realized that his family no longer enjoyed the safety and security of their Nazareth home. They were a family on the run.

We don't know how long Joseph, Mary, and Jesus stayed in Egypt—a few months or several years. But when the danger had passed, an angel again appeared to Joseph in a dream and told him to take Mary and Jesus back to the land of Israel. The Gospel writer recounts four dreams of Joseph in the opening chapter of Matthew's Gospel. Through each dream, God gave Joseph direction as he sought God's will. In each instance, Joseph responded obediently, and through his choices God prepared the way for the mission of his Son. Following the path of his ancient ancestors under Moses, Joseph led his family from Egypt into the land of Israel.

Joseph had been appropriately named after Joseph, the patriarch of the Book of Genesis. That ancient Joseph also was a dreamer and an interpreter of dreams. He, too, had saved his family from destruction by bringing them into Egypt to escape a famine in Israel. The more ancient Joseph had provided for his family in exile, so that many years later, under the leadership of Moses, they could make that long journey through the desert and back to the land of God's promise.

Joseph of Nazareth served as an important link between the Old Testament and the New. He was steeped in the faith of Israel, followed the traditions of his ancestors, Joseph, Moses, and David, and set the stage for the coming of Jesus to this ancient people.

Our own experience of returning home from a long journey can give us a glimpse of the joy that Joseph must have felt as he and his family arrived back in Nazareth. Most people agree that "there's no place like home," but few people know the unspeakable joy felt by refugees when they return to their homeland after years of exile. For millions of refugees today, however, there will be no return during their lifetime. Forced to flee because of political danger, the modern refugee, more often than not, is in permanent exile. For so many people, the longing for home is often just a dream. Joseph was able to return home, but he kept in his heart the experience of exile. For that reason, people through the centuries have looked to Joseph as the patron saint of refugees and immigrants, the protector of those who have been deprived of their homes, and the protector of those who travel from their homeland to new homes.

Pilgrim

Joseph willingly took another form of travel many times during his life: the journey of pilgrimage. There were three annual pilgrimage festivals during the days of Jerusalem's temple: the Feasts of Passover, Pentecost, and Tabernacles. Each of these celebrated some aspect of Israel's ancient history. Though the feasts could be observed at home, many Jews would travel to Jerusalem to take part in the feast at the temple. As a pilgrim, Joseph left his individual home to go to the house of God, the temple, where all people could find a home.

Joseph and his family must have traveled often to the city of Jerusalem. The journey was long, requiring several days. Since travel was dangerous, families would always make the journey with their extended families or they would join a caravan with hired guards. These pilgrimages were not solemn events but filled, instead, with much singing, dancing, and feasting. They were celebrations of God's goodness— no need for somber piety here. Adults and children alike eagerly awaited the feasts.

One of these, the Feast of Tabernacles, was an autumn festival associated with the olive and grape harvest. A special Sabbath marked the beginning of the seven-day feast. With the difficult work of harvest complete, the people rested, rejoiced, ate, drank, danced, sang, and generally celebrated. They built temporary shelters—a type of hut or tabernacle—in which to eat and sleep during the days of the festival. The shelters reminded them of the days of their ancestors, who had wandered through the desert for forty years while living in tents or temporary huts.

Joseph built one of these tabernacles each year near his family's home in Nazareth. Here he, Mary, and Jesus would camp out each evening, sharing their meals, rejoicing with their neighbors, and reclining at bedtime while looking up at the stars peeking through the scattered branches covering the fragile hut.

Occasionally, Joseph's family would travel to Jerusalem to celebrate the feast as pilgrims. Jews from Palestine and from countries throughout the

Roman world would flock to Jerusalem. Along the trails winding through the land resounded the songs of the festive travelers. People could feel in Jerusalem during the festival days the pulse of the entire Jewish people. They could meet in the street every type of Jew from every corner of the world and learn how they lived. Every Jew who did not live in Israel was considered a dispersed Jew, a Diaspora Jew. They were away from the home of all Jews: Jerusalem. A Jew like Joseph was more at home at the temple of Jerusalem than anywhere else on earth.

On the slopes surrounding Jerusalem, Joseph would set up a tabernacle because there was no room to house all the pilgrims within the city walls. Jesus, Mary, and Joseph would enter the city to mingle among their fellow Jews costumed in colorful clothing depicting the culture of their native places. They would sing and dance in the courtyards and open spaces of the city.

Throughout the crowded city, people would carry palm leaves and fruits, and in every corner of the city, vendors sold food and drink from huts made of olive branches. The last event of the evening, the torch dance, continued late into the night.

Living in temporary shelter for a week served as a vivid reminder of those who lived in huts or were homeless throughout their lives. It was a reminder that even one's home was not truly permanent. The unstable huts distinctly demonstrated the temporary quality and the uncertainty of all of life. In this life we are always on a journey that anticipates our arrival at our promised eternal home.

Luke's Gospel gives us an account of a pilgrim feast Joseph's family attended when Jesus was twelve years old. Passover was the most important pilgrim feast of the time, and it seems that Joseph and Mary made the journey to Jerusalem for the event every year. We do not know if Jesus always went with them, but we do know that he went with them during this important transitional year in his religious development. According to Jewish custom, Jesus, at twelve, was ready to accept responsibility for the Torah and its moral and ritual commands. Later Jewish tradition would ritualize this transition in a child's life by the bar mitzvah.

The streets of Jerusalem swelled with pilgrims during the week of Passover. Roads built by imperial Rome made travel easy. The pilgrims numbered in the hundreds of thousands, from all places in which Jews dwelt throughout the Roman world. They came from Syria, Asia Minor, Babylon, Greece, Egypt, and Rome. Approaching the city from the surrounding hills, the pilgrims sang psalms of praise to God: "I rejoiced when they said to me, Let us go up to the House of the Lord.... Let us go up to Zion, to the House of our God.... It is better to spend one day in God's courts than a thousand elsewhere.... How beautiful is your dwelling, O Lord our God.... My spirit longs for the courts of the Lord."

The Passover ritual originally was a home ritual, then it became a temple ritual. But in the days of Joseph, it was both. On the afternoon before Passover, Joseph would purchase a lamb from the market and bring it to the temple to have it slaughtered. He would then take it to the home or inn where they were staying, roast it, and eat it that evening with his extended family. It was necessary to form a group of family or friends of at least ten people for the Passover meal, for the very practical reason that it took at least ten people to eat a whole roasted lamb in one sitting.

Throughout the world outside of Jerusalem, Jewish families celebrated the Passover in their homes with ceremonies almost identical to the Seder observed by Jews today. They mixed strong wine with water and drank it from ceremonial cups, and they ate bitter herbs and other traditional foods of the Passover with newly baked, unleavened bread. The narrative of the festival recounted

God's deliverance of the Israelites from the slavery of Egypt and all the redemptive events of that night of all nights. The meal concluded with joyful singing and a final blessing. Wherever in the world Jews celebrate Passover, the moon is always full on that night, and Jews feel more at home with God than on any other night of the year.

After eating the sacrificial meal, Joseph and his family would have gone back outside, where the bright moon cast a silvery gleam over the flat roofs of the city. Again the streets of Jerusalem were filled with promenading Jews, natives and pilgrims side by side. Joseph and his family would move from one group to another, greeting friends and making new ones. By this hour, the priests would have opened the gates of the Holy House, as the temple was called, where Jesus, Mary, and Joseph would spend the rest of the night along with thousands of other pilgrims, praying and singing hymns of praise to God.

At the conclusion of the festival, Joseph packed his traveling bags and joined the caravan of Nazarenes for the long journey back home. After a day's journey, as they settled down for the night, Joseph and Mary searched for their adolescent son, assuming he had been in the caravan with his cousins and friends. When they could not find him, they were afraid that he was lost among the pilgrims back in Jerusalem. They frantically searched the city and found him in the temple, talking with the teachers of Israel, who were amazed at his wisdom. Joseph and Mary were astonished, angry, and bewildered. "Your father and I have been anxiously searching for you. Why have you done this?" Jesus replied in a way they did not understand: "Did you not know that I must be in my Father's house?"

"My Father's house" referred to the temple and all associated with God's dwelling on earth. This is the first time in the Gospels that Jesus calls God his Father. *Abba,* the affectionate term that Jesus used for Joseph, he now used to designate his eternal Father. Joseph began to realize that his son's life would not be focused on the carpentry trade, that perhaps his son was destined for something much bigger than Nazareth could offer. The home in Nazareth would no longer be the center of his son's world; rather, the house of God and all the concerns of his Father God would consume his mind and heart.

Yet by no means did the fatherhood of Joseph end at that moment. The Gospel goes on to relate that Jesus returned to Nazareth with his parents and was obedient to them. Like any Jewish child of the time, Jesus honored his father, responded to his instructions, and respected his paternal authority throughout his life. The home of Joseph and the house of God did not compete for the attention of Jesus. He honored both houses by living as son of Joseph and Son of God.

You Can't Go Home Again

As has often been said, "You can't go home again."
Sometimes in adult life, we return to the place
where we grew up, trying to recapture the happiness and simplicity of our youth, only to be disap-
pointed. We cannot return to our family home and
find things as they used to be. Old houses and
buildings get torn down and replaced by new ones.
Old friends move away or die. Children are born,
new families move into the neighborhood, and
past relationships never remain the same.

Scripture suggests that Jesus experienced this
kind of nostalgic disappointment and heartache
when he made the twenty-eight-mile trek to
Nazareth as an adult (see Mark 6:1). Jesus had
made his home in the seaside town of Capernaum,
where he lived with Peter and Andrew. This is the
only place in the Gospel where Jesus is said to be "at
home" (Mark 2:1). We can assume that Peter and
Andrew's wives and extended family also lived there

because Jesus healed the mother of Peter's wife there (see Mark 1:29-31).

One of the most obvious changes in Jesus' home place was that Joseph had died. We don't know when he died, but Joseph is not mentioned in Scripture after the account of the Passover pilgrimage when Jesus was twelve. Had Joseph been alive during Jesus' adult ministry, it would have been natural to speak of him, since Mary is mentioned several times after Jesus is grown. But many other things in Jesus' life had changed as well. Relationships and expectations would never be the same.

Jesus was not well received when he returned to preach in the synagogue of Nazareth. His words were unexpected and challenging. The people asked, "Is this not the carpenter's son?" (Matthew 13:55). They had expected Jesus to be the same as when he was younger, but like all of us, Jesus had changed. No longer the submissive child, the playful youth they had known, Jesus was a man with a mission. He had a burning desire to do the will of his Father, to change people's hearts and transform their lives. But not only did the townspeople resist Jesus, they took him to the brow of the hill on which Nazareth was built and tried to throw him off the cliff (see Luke 4:29). Jesus left his hometown for the last time with a heavy and homesick heart.

If it is true that we can't go home again, then perhaps we must learn to carry our homes with us in our souls. This home that we carry is our collection of memories, lessons learned and confidence gained, triumphs and trials, affirmations and criticisms, nurture and challenge. We must in fact go back to this home often. This wise, confident, secure, and protected place in the heart goes with us wherever we travel.

5

$\mathcal{H}$ome-Builder:
Husband, Father, and Laborer

$\mathcal{M}$ore than bricks and mortar, four walls and a roof, a home is made up of the relationships among the people who live within the structure. Joseph was a home-builder not only because he built homes for a living, but also because he was committed to the loving relationships that made up his home. Home-building is hard work physically, emotionally, and spiritually. A house does not automatically become a home. We build our homes brick by brick, experience by experience, through trial and error, triumphs and failures, mistakes and forgiveness. The architectural plans and blueprints give us a helpful beginning, but the real work of home-building is a labor of the spirit. The best plans do not become reality without lots of toil, struggle, and patient endurance.

Husband

We might think that Joseph and Mary were the proverbial match made in heaven, that their daily lives were filled with bliss in every imaginable way. We project our idealistic images of love on this saintly couple and assume they must have had the best of all possible relationships. But a realistic look at their lives reveals a different picture.

As the Gospel of Matthew begins, we find Joseph in a painful predicament. Just as he was preparing for the marriage feast to receive his bride into his home, he discovered that Mary, his betrothed, was pregnant. Imagine the sorrow, anger, and embarrassment Joseph must have experienced as he realized that his beloved was bearing a child before he had begun to live with her. Joseph was, of course, the only one besides Mary who knew that he was not the father of the child. What a predicament!

Jewish marriages in the time of Joseph and Mary took place in two stages. The first stage, called the betrothal, was the formal exchange of consent, made at the home of the bride's father. The second stage, made some months or even years later, was the formal transfer of the bride to the house of the groom. Joseph and Mary had already completed the first stage. Their betrothal was a legally contracted marriage, and Joseph and Mary were considered husband and wife, bound by matrimonial fidelity. But they had not yet entered the second stage in which they would begin to live together.

Joseph knew that Mary was an honorable woman. Yet he also knew that pregnancy could only be the result of either her willing or forced relations with a man. Since in ancient Israel the betrothal was a true marriage covenant, Joseph could only assume that his new wife had committed adultery or been raped. The legal punishment for adultery was stoning. Joseph would have been within his rights to humiliate her publicly and charge her with adultery. But Joseph was a good man and loved his wife dearly; he certainly did not want her to endure a harsh punishment and public disgrace. He decided to give her the prescribed document of divorce privately.

Joseph's agonizing choice was cut short when an angel appeared to him in a dream to let him in on what God had in mind. Most of us probably think it would be rather wonderful to be touched by an angel. But if the truth be told, angels are trouble-makers. They usually come from God with a message that takes a neat and tidy life and turns everything upside down. Nearly every angelic en-counter in the Old Testament radically upends lives. Joseph knew the biblical stories well, and an angelic encounter did not set his heart aglow with sweet sentiment. He was scared. He began to wonder how much stress and anguish he would have to endure in order to accomplish God's will.

"Do not be afraid to take Mary as your wife, for the child conceived in her is from the Holy Spirit," said the angel. What was that? Conceived from the Holy Spirit? Joseph had been so looking forward to a normal married life. But God had other ideas. Joseph did not have any clear understanding of the kind of married life that lay ahead. The purpose of his matrimonial vocation would gradually unfold through the years. Yet, like Mary, Joseph accepted and responded favorably to the movements of God's Spirit within him.

So there was no need to cancel the wedding plans. Joseph would organize a wedding feast for the day when he would bring Mary to live in his home. The day would be marked by joy and celebration, eating and drinking, music and dancing.

Following the feast, the couple would be led in a torch-lit procession from the home of Mary's parents to the home that Joseph had prepared for his bride. After crossing the threshold, the rest of the young couple's lives would be filled with the same kinds of joys and pains, successes and disappointments that characterize every marriage.

All married couples struggle to build a home together. When we get married, it's a good thing we're not able to anticipate all the challenges that life will bring. We probably wouldn't have the guts to accept them. But in the midst of the struggles of marriage, Joseph can teach us and assist us. Like all newly married people, Joseph was hoping for a pleasant and enjoyable life. But his life demonstrates that embracing sacrifice and giving generously can lead to greater joy and fulfillment than can be imagined when promising fidelity on the wedding day: "For better, for worse, for richer, for poorer, in sickness and in health." When a couple pledge their love, there is no way to know or control the future. Joseph teaches us that accepting and living in the service of God's plan does not cost us our happiness, but rather guarantees it.

Father

The fatherhood of Joseph began under unusual circumstances, to say the least. His child was conceived, though not by his own doing. Yet Joseph was not merely a caretaker for Jesus, he was truly his father. The gospels make it clear that Joseph was not the biological parent of Jesus, but they do not hesitate to call Joseph his father. Luke's narrative of Jesus' infancy and adolescence repeatedly refers to Joseph as Jesus' father (2:33, 48) and parent (2:27, 41, 43, 48).

Jewish law based paternity on a man's willingness to acknowledge a child as his own. Joseph expressed his willingness to claim Jesus as his own by taking Mary into his home as his wife during her pregnancy, and by giving Jesus his name. In this way, Joseph assumed public responsibility for Mary and the child and claimed all the rights and responsibilities of a father. Thus, according to the law of Israel, Joseph was the authentic father of Jesus.

To all in Nazareth, Joseph's fatherhood was normal in every way. He caressed his infant son in his arms, held the laughing baby high in the air, and bounced his playful boy on his knees. As Jesus grew, Joseph taught him to play games, to do his chores, and to respect his mother. In turn, Jesus loved and honored Joseph as his father, with all the respect stipulated by the ancient commandment to honor mother and father. The young Jesus looked into Joseph's eyes for reassurance, looked to his smile for confidence, and listened to his words to grow in trust.

During the childhood years of Jesus, his father had the primary responsibility for his religious education. Joseph taught Jesus the stories of their creative and protective God. He brought him to the brow of the hill and showed him the vast land that God had given his ancestors. He taught him about the wide and wonderful world that stretched out beyond their hillside village as they watched the merchants and soldiers passing through the valley below. Jesus accompanied his father to the synagogue, where he learned to read and study the Scriptures of Israel and to discuss the ancient traditions.

An important duty of any father in those days was to teach his son his trade. Joseph taught Jesus to saw and lathe, hammer and screw, sharpen and grind, chisel and drill. During most of his early life, Jesus worked by his earthly father's side as an apprentice at his workbench. But Joseph taught his son much more than skilled labor. He taught him the dignity of work, the importance of quality, the value of honesty, and the importance of using his talents well.

The relationship of father and son was so clear to

the people of Nazareth that when Jesus returned as an adult, the people asked, "Is this not Joseph's son?" (Luke 4:22). Throughout history, Joseph has been called the father of Jesus, but with various adjectival prefixes: foster, adoptive, putative, assumed, matrimonial, vicarious, legal. But his identity was clear to Jesus, who called him *Abba,* or Dad.

All infants need to be held and played with, looked at and made to laugh, cradled and rocked, as if they were the only ones in the world. Children need to know that they are not accidental, unwanted, or a burden, and that they are cherished, treasured, and loved unconditionally. Every adolescent needs to be affirmed, told that she is smart and beautiful, that he is competent and strong. When children reach the age where they seem to need their parents less, we can be assured that they need us more than ever.

All parents suffer from an occasional lack of confidence in their ability. We worry that we don't have enough patience, stability, strength, or wisdom. We feel inadequate sometimes for the overwhelming task of raising a child. Joseph can teach us to trust in God who will supply those qualities that we seem to lack. Joseph discovered in his own experience that when God chooses a person for a task, God always provides the means to carry it out.

Joseph is a mentor for all sorts of fathers. For men who are biological fathers, he serves as a model of responsibility in accepting the privilege of caring for, providing for, protecting, and educating their children. For men who are called to other kinds of fatherhood—stepfathers, adoptive fathers, and foster fathers—Joseph models generous, accepting love. He was the man of the hour when his son's life was imperiled in Bethlehem and Egypt. Joseph, the protector, can inspire fathers to go to any length to protect, guard, and defend their children. Protecting, providing, educating, encouraging, and affirming children is the task of a father.

Joseph will inspire any dad who seeks his counsel to appreciate the incredible gift of fatherhood.

Laborer

Making a living in Nazareth was difficult. Industry of any kind was almost nonexistent. Even if Nazareth had produced a commodity for trade or export, transporting that product to potential buyers would have been quite challenging. Most of the people of Nazareth worked the land. Joseph was probably the only carpenter in town.

The gospels describe the trade of Joseph as a *tekton*. This Greek word implies a profession that was a bit more diverse than our word "carpenter" suggests. Perhaps best translated as craftsman, the word denotes a person who works in wood or stone. Joseph was probably the all-purpose village craftsman. Among the tools in his workshop were the hammer, saw, chisel, lathe, plane, mallet, ruler, and square.

He made everything from the agricultural

implements of area farmers—like yokes, plows, threshing sledges, and winnowing forks—to houses and furniture for the villagers. In building houses, Joseph laid foundation stones, formed doors and door frames, and hoisted roof beams. He also made furniture such as tables, stools, lamp stands, and beds, as well as storage items such as chests, cabinets, and boxes.

As a person who built houses throughout his life, Joseph knew the importance of quality construction. He was a trustworthy contractor. He built his reputation on work well done and a village full of satisfied customers. But Joseph knew that a house was more than carefully constructed stone, frame, and wood beams. He often repeated to himself the words of his ancestors, "Unless the Lord builds the house, those who build it labor in vain" (Psalm 127:1).

Paintings of Joseph from later ages frequently depict him as an old man, but he was probably young and strong during Jesus' childhood. His profession demanded that he be fit and muscular. He usually worked outside, either in the courtyard or making house repairs for the villagers. During slow periods in Nazareth, Joseph might have traveled back and forth to Sepphoris, four miles away. Sepphoris was being rebuilt in grand style and Joseph and son may have signed on as skilled laborers for the city's many construction projects.

As a skilled tradesman, Joseph's work offered a bit more predictability than the work of the farmers, whose livelihoods depended on the seasons and the weather. Yet in an age before workers' compensation and retirement investing, Joseph still lived insecurely and perilously close to the edge. He received his wages primarily through barter—a bushel of vegetables for a repaired plow, a couple of goats for a wooden cabinet. Sometimes he earned a silver denarius for a day's labor. He provided his family with shelter and food, but they probably had little beyond the basics.

Joseph's hard work six days every week teaches us the dignity of human labor. The working day is not the part of life that we have to endure before the real life of the weekend or vacation begins. Rather, Joseph's example encourages us to find the meaning of life in our daily tasks. Otherwise, we will not find it at all.

Joseph did not have to worry about the constant feeling of inadequacy fostered by our modern consumerist culture and advertising. Mary and Jesus did not hound him about what they could not afford to have. Rather, Joseph was blessed to live in an age in which families were grateful for a moderate income and the basic necessities of life. He taught his family to trust and believe that with their own work and effort, God would provide for their needs.

Because he was a wise home-builder, Joseph can offer us a more balanced and gracious view of money and time, work and leisure. He teaches us that we can find God and become holy in the midst of the work we do each day. Through our daily work, we enjoy the privilege of sharing in the creating work of God. The One who created the world and holds all things in existence, charges us to be stewards of our world and our homes.

6

$\mathcal{A}$ Saintly Mentor Through the Cycles of Life

$\mathcal{Y}$ ou've probably heard at one time or other a version of the "That's good, that's bad" story. Something a person thought was bad turns out to be good, and what was thought to be good is actually bad. In the opening chapters of the New Testament, Joseph's life with Jesus and Mary reads this way. His adventures alternate between sorrow and joy, a repeated experience of "That's bad, no, that's good."

When we meet Joseph in the Bible, he is in a

painful predicament. He has just discovered that Mary is pregnant and he is not the father. Oh, that's bad....

No, that's good, because Joseph then discerns in a dream that the conception of Mary's son was a wondrous work of God and that Joseph is part of God's plan (see Matthew 1:18-21).

When the time for the birth of Jesus arrives, Joseph and his wife are away from home. He searches for an appropriate place for the delivery but can find no room except in a place where animals lodge. Oh, that's bad....

No, that's good, because all his anxiety turns to wonder as Mary safely delivers a son and the shepherds come to see this marvelous child lying in a manger (see Luke 2:6-7).

Eight days later, it is time for the circumcision of the child, according to Jewish tradition. Joseph experiences the pain of his new son and listens to his fearful cry. Oh, that's bad....

No, that's good, because at that moment, Joseph's son joins the people of the covenant and Joseph gives the child the name Jesus (see Luke 2:21).

When Joseph brings Jesus up to the temple in Jerusalem for the ancient ritual of the child's presentation, a prophet named Simeon tells of painful days to come. Simeon tells Mary that her son will bring great upheaval in Israel and be opposed by many, and that a sword of sorrow will pierce her soul. Oh, that's bad....

No that's good, because from that suffering great things will be accomplished. Simeon praises God for bringing salvation through this child, who will be light and glory for all people (see Luke 2:28-35).

When King Herod hears of Jesus' birth, he begins to search for Jesus in order to have him killed. Joseph receives a message in a dream to flee with his child into Egypt. Oh, that's bad....

No, that's good, because although Herod puts to death all the male children in Bethlehem in an attempt to kill the royal child, Jesus escapes danger and is safe in a place of refuge (see Matthew 2:13-16).

Later, when Herod dies, God instructs Joseph in a dream to make the dangerous journey from Egypt back into the land of Israel. Oh, that's bad....

No, that's good, because like his ancestors, Joseph brings Jesus out of Egypt into the land of God's promise. Joseph takes Jesus to Nazareth, where he makes his home and raises Jesus (see Matthew 2:19-23).

Several years later, Joseph brings his family to Jerusalem for the annual feast. Later, as they return home, Joseph and Mary discover that Jesus is not with their relatives in the traveling party. They frantically search for their child, who they believe is lost in the large city. Oh, that's bad....

No, that's good, because they find Jesus in the temple among the teachers. As Jesus says he must be in his Father's house, Joseph begins to realize the great but mysterious destiny in store for his child.

The saga of Joseph can teach us about the ways

God works in human life. All of life presents us with movement from bad to good, from sorrow to joy. Our lives are a cyclical experience of the mystery of Jesus' saving life, his burial in the earth, and his rising to new life.

Perhaps the burial of the statue of Joseph upside down in the ground and the restoration of his image right-side up in a new home ritualize this bad-to-good, sorrow-to-joy cycle of life. Moving from a home and putting it up for sale can be a difficult and sad process. But moving into a new house and making it a home can be joyful and renewing. Living the life of faith helps us see more clearly how joy can come out of pain. For the one who trusts, suffering and sorrow never mark the end of the story.

Devotion to the Saints

I've always believed that when people die they do not cease to exist. I believe people enter another state that is free of the time and space restrictions of earthbound existence. But I never gave much thought to the most practical consequence of that rather abstract belief: the idea that those who share the joys of the next life have a personal interest in our welfare. Who could be in a better position to help me in my needs than a saint of God?

I used to think of contact and communication with the dead as something I wanted no part of. I associated it with the occult and sorcery, a strange spiritualism that I still choose to avoid. But the possibility of inviting the saints to help me and intercede for me has changed my thinking. Now I realize that nothing could be more natural and normal than a relationship with someone who is fully alive in God. The saints' heavenly existence has relieved them of all the narrow selfishness that sometimes characterizes our lives on earth; so why would they not have a vital and loving interest in me?

Saints are ordinary people who lived ordinary lives in an extraordinary way. They understand all the struggles and anxieties of earthly existence since they lived it themselves. They know what it was like to work each day, to raise children, to struggle at marriage, to worry about finances. There is a long history of saints who have been more than ordinarily involved with the community of believers in this world through miracles and special favors. Why shouldn't I be one of those enjoying the blessings of a caring saint?

Christians call this continuity between people in this life and those in eternal life the "communion of saints." It is the belief that we continue in relationship with those who have passed on to the next life, that personal relationships transcend time and space, that we are all part of the same family, the family of God.

All of us have a deep longing to be loved, to be understood and accepted as we are. We desire union with others; we fear loneliness and isolation. The union between the people of the earth and the saints in heaven is real. We don't just remember and admire the saints as we do historical figures. We can read biographies about historical characters and imitate their lives but the relationships we can have with the saints goes well beyond that. Not only can we know about them, we can truly know them. They are alive, though in a different way than we are, and their union with us is real, though not in a sensory way. Not only are *we* interested in *their* lives, *they* are vitally interested in *ours.*

We belong to a community much larger than the one we can see. Most of the time, seeing is believing, but at other times, believing is seeing. If we believe what people have believed for centuries and what the biblical writers teach us, then we might begin to see this larger community of heavenly companions. We see the saints not with our physical eyes, but with the eyes of our spirit, which are insightful enough to see beyond our visible world.

Cultivating friendship with a saint is not that different from cultivating friendship in this world. We look for things we have in common. If a saint's life and interests are similar to our own, we are more likely to hit it off. Sometimes a friendship in the world develops a spiritual dimension characterized by intimate discussion and prayer. In the communion of saints, a saint can become that kind of soul mate.

People who are not familiar with this concept of spiritual friendship sometimes object. "Can't I just go straight to God? Aren't you putting other mediators in the way to God? After all, the New Testament says that Jesus is the only mediator between God and humanity" (see 1 Timothy 2:5). True, but even Jesus enlisted help to bring people to God. He chose apostles to assist him during his earthly life and to continue his work after he departed. Those disciples became saints and now they're still helping Jesus bring people to God. Peter, Andrew, James, and John still have a job to do after all these years.

The New Testament writers continually urge the

followers of Jesus to pray for each other. "Pray for me to the Lord, says Simon Peter" (Acts 8:24). "Brothers and sisters, pray for us," Paul asks (2 Thessa-lonians 3:1). "Pray for one another," advises James (James 5:16). When we read about the early church, it's clear that it was not made up of solitary individuals praying to God alone. It was a community of prayer, with everyone praying for one another, lifting up this need and that need to God. And what better prayer partners than those who are in the closest possible union with God in heaven? When I ask my friends on earth or my friends in heaven to pray for me in matters large and small, I am simply express-ing solidarity with my companions in the family of God, for "the prayer of the righteous is powerful and effective" (James 5:16). We are not alone. We need one another.

A Mentor for the Twenty-First Century

St. Joseph of heaven is really the same person as Joseph of Nazareth. He is an ideal mentor in areas that we can relate to—earning a living, choosing a spouse, cultivating a marriage, raising a child, creating a home, dealing with an adolescent, integrating prayer into daily life, honoring God in family life.

Long neglected among the community of believers, St. Joseph is making a comeback. He is a saint for the twenty-first century. As we struggle to create peaceful, happy, holy, and creative homes, we have a heavenly friend in Joseph of Nazareth. The example of his life directs us to the heart of what makes life fulfilling and gives it meaning.

Too often, we picture St. Joseph with a halo on his head and hands folded on his chest. The real man wouldn't recognize himself in this image. Joseph was a rugged, confident, and honest man of great personal integrity. He knew what his life was about, and he was relentless in his devotion to his family. We can surmise that Joseph was open to his emotions, that he laughed heartily and was not afraid to cry. He worked hard but he knew how to celebrate with singing and dancing. He was the kind of man with whom any good woman would want to share her life, the kind of man any child would love to call Dad.

We need healthy male role models these days, and they don't come any better than Joseph. Our society has been described as father-hungry. We have too many absent fathers, deadbeat dads, daughters without fathers to encourage them, and sons without dads to look up to. Many fathers are either authoritarian and overbearing, or weak and passive. For the father-hungry people of the world, for the millions deprived of a healthy, fulfilling relationship with a father, Joseph is an ideal foster father. When we need the attention that only a father can give, the man that Jesus called Dad is ready to listen.

7

Domestic Devotion to St. Joseph

*D*evotion to St. Joseph involves several elements: honoring Joseph for the kind of life he led on earth, adopting him as a mentor for our own lives, developing a personal relationship with him, and asking him to pray for us in our earthly needs.

Devotion to St. Joseph is a totally different kind of honor than the honor we give to God. Even God honors the saints. As Jesus said, "Whoever serves me, the Father will honor" (John 12:26). We can honor an Olympic champion with a gold medal and a ticker tape parade, but the glory belongs to God, as many champions acknowledge. We can honor Joseph with admiration and devotion, but we adore and worship God alone. Devotion to Joseph goes wrong when it became idolatry, when it fixates on the saint in place of God. Genuine devotion to Joseph always moves through him to a richer relationship with Jesus and a more profound worship of God.

Because we are still earthly creatures, we relate to invisible reality through earthly things. In the same way that a photograph or a portrait reminds us of a loved one, pictures, icons, medals, and statues remind us of our heavenly companions. The statue of St. Joseph on my mantel is a constant reminder of his heroic life and of my desire to imitate his qualities. Because I am developing a deeper friendship with Joseph, a frequent look at his image in my living room helps me.

But images are simply reminders, nothing more.

They are like photographs we keep of an absent friend. We might look at the picture and think of our friend, or keep it before us when we talk to the friend on the phone. But talking to the photo instead of our friend, or thinking that the photo is actually our friend, would be disordered. It's the same with statues and images of the saints. They can remind us of the saint or help us focus our attention in prayer, but they don't have any power in themselves. Devotion is directed toward the real person, the saint in the life of heaven.

For the same reason that images are significant for us, rituals are also important. For a friendship to be real, we need smiles, laughter, embraces, and all the other gestures that help us to "feel" a relationship rather than to just "know" it in our head. We also crave ways to feel and experience spiritual realities. We know the more traditional sacramental rituals of Christianity, like sharing bread and wine, being bathed in water, and being anointed with oil.

But any human action, like planting a flower garden, baking fresh bread, or lighting a candle, can be an occasion to experience a heavenly reality.

Devotion or Superstition

The ritual of burying a statue of St. Joseph in the ground to implore a domestic blessing is not deeply rooted in Christian history and has no official endorsement by any church. No one knows where or how it began. Maybe it has become wildly popular because it has not been regulated or officially sanctioned by any institutional body. Lots of people in many places have simply found it a meaningful ritual in which to experience a blessing from God. There is no right or wrong way of doing it and there is no guarantee of its success. Because it is uncontrolled, the same action can be either an irreverent superstition or a faith-filled devotion.

So what is the difference? Superstition or devotion? Believing that the statue or the ritual causes a good effect is superstition. Using the statue to get what we want, just by saying the right prayer or performing the right action, is more like casting a spell than like a prayerful devotion. The effects depend not on the object and ritual but the persons involved: those performing the prayerful ritual and heavenly Joseph himself. When people direct their confident prayers to God, they get results. Objects, images, words, and rituals dispose a person to the invisible grace God wants to give.

A statue of St. Joseph is not a good-luck charm; it is an object of devotion. The person seeking to honor St. Joseph should choose an appropriate image. Whether it be a Byzantine icon, a Latino wood-carved *santo,* an alabaster statue, or a plastic dashboard figurine is a matter of taste. And as the saying goes, it's no use arguing taste.

Concerning the method, it doesn't matter if the statue is upside-down, near the "for sale" sign, in the backyard, in the front yard, facing the house, or facing the street. St. Joseph must smile at our human tendency to obsess about these issues. He doesn't really care. He doesn't even care if he's buried. The ritual is for us poor creatures.

Will your house sell if you bury a statue of St. Joseph in your yard? I don't know. I do know that he is a great mentor, and I know that he wants to help you accomplish God's will for your life. He is a great partner in prayer, and wonderful things have happened in the lives of people who developed a friendship with this manly saint.

I do recommend this: If you bury a statue of Joseph in the ground, let your life be characterized by trust, prayer, and faithfulness. Superstition is a selfish act; devotion is an act of generosity. I would suggest that the prayerful ritual of a couple whose lives are characterized by devoted love, daily prayer, and generous giving is more likely to result in a sold house than the same ritual performed by a wealthy developer seeking to make a profit.

But who knows? St. Joseph has a sense of humor and loves to teach us lessons that impact our lives. The stories told by people who have buried statues of Joseph are legion.

A Realtor for All Seasons

A religious goods store owner reported that he sells thousands of St. Joseph statues and can hardly keep them in stock. St. Joseph outsells his biggest competitor, his spouse Mary, five to one. The merchant said that he has witnessed the phenomenon for the past twenty years, but this year has seen the most sales ever.

People buy St. Joseph statues in all sizes, from the foot-tall detailed image to the three-inch plastic model. Sometimes the size of the statue depends on the time of year. In the summer, people dig with shovels and bury larger statues. But when the ground is frozen and people are chipping out holes with pickaxes, the smaller variety seems more appropriate.

A number of the infamous St. Joseph home sale kits are on the market. There are different versions, but most come with a three-inch plastic statue and some form of instructions. One package even includes a waterproof burying bag. The enclosed prayer in one kit begins with what sounds like a threat: "We know you don't like to be buried upside down, but..."

Newspapers and magazines throughout the country have carried stories on the phenomenon of St. Joseph. "Don't be surprised," noted the *Wall Street Journal,* "if one dark night you spot your neighbors digging a hole and burying a statue of St. Joseph. They're only seeking a little saintly assistance in a buyers' market." The *Baltimore Sun* began its report thus: "Burying a small statue of St. Joseph headfirst next to the house may be a last-ditch attempt by home sellers, but there are enough success stories to consider the holy man for Realtor of the Year."

Other recent headlines include: "Bury Saint Joe,

Wait for Offers" (*Arizona Republic*); "Underground Agent, St. Joseph Holds out Hope for Home Sellers" (*Chicago Tribune*); "Tough Sale? Put a Saint on the Case" (*The Oregonian*); and "Saintly Sales Agent Going Underground" (*Colorado Springs Gazette Telegraph*).

The practice of burying St. Joseph is apparently widely promoted among real estate agents. A Century 21 Realtor buys her statues several dozen at a time for her clients. Many realtors have "believe it or not" stories. Some even provide information about the practice on their websites.

But as every agent would advise, don't forget to do the practical things to sell the house, such as cleaning the carpets, painting the trim, and setting a reasonable price. Then for good measure, just to make sure your intentions are honorable, why not promise to give a percentage of your proceeds from the sale to an organization for the homeless, or to those who work with victims of domestic violence and abuse?

Since selling my home under the patronage of Joseph the Realtor, I feel like I have joined a special club, a loose network of people who have similar stories to tell. My friend Deb, in New Orleans, recalls her experience from many years ago: "My husband left home unexpectedly when our boys were in second and third grades. While battling my feelings of rejection and abandonment, I faced taking care of them while finding a job with my high-school education. One of the many tasks at hand was selling our family home. At first, few people looked at it and fewer displayed interest. Someone told me to bury a statue of St. Joseph in the yard, a suggestion I found horrifying. But desperate people do desperate things, and I figured St. Joseph wouldn't really mind.... So I buried him. And I sold the house a few days later. After we had moved to our older, smaller house, I took the statue of St. Joseph that I had buried in the yard, cleaned him off, and put him in a place of honor in our new home. I placed little school pictures of each boy at the base of the statue and told Joseph that he would have to take over as honorary dad. The boys are in their twenties now, but I still have talks with Joseph when I think either son needs a little nudge!"

My friend Kathleen recently put her house up for sale in St. Paul in order to move to Mystic, Connecticut. After she had been waiting several months for an offer, a workmate gave her a statue of Joseph. I recently e-mailed her to ask about how the sale was going. Here is her reply: "That playful fellow St. Joseph finally did come through. We ended up selling the house (for the third time) to the first person who'd bought it. Long story. I guess Somebody wanted me to learn a bit more about 'letting go.' Obviously, Joe's got a puckish sense of humor. And here I'd always considered him boring and staid!"

There's a story moving around the Internet that sounds like an urban legend, but having experienced the rascally humor of Joseph, I can't be sure.

"There was a seller who bought a St. Joseph statue and was very excited; he just knew that his home would sell for sure now. He planted it in the back-yard, waited a couple of weeks, but nothing happened. He planted it in the front yard, waited another couple of weeks, and still nothing happened. He planted it in front of the yard sign, waited, and nothing happened. He then planted it in the side yard, waited, and still nothing happened.

This went on for over three months. His yard was full of holes from planting and replanting St. Joseph. After three months the seller was frustrated and threw St. Joseph in the trash. A few days later the frustrated seller opened the newspaper and saw the headline, 'Local Dump Has Been Sold.'"

Saint for a New Age

I have had great fun in developing a devotion to my new heavenly friend, Joseph of Nazareth. There can be great joy in cultivating a friendship with someone whose goodness and heroism is acknowledged officially by the community of believers throughout the world.

Some time back, probably during the Age of Enlightenment, we cut much of the joy and celebration out of religion. But union with the people of heaven is not just about folded hands, bowed head, and cautious living. As twenty-first-century believers, it's time to take back what we have lost. And I don't think there is anyone better suited to lead the way back to heavenly fun, faith, and friendship than that humorous, playful, loving, and confident guy, St. Joseph.

The final lesson that Joseph has taught me is that ultimately we are all called to be saints. That is the purpose and goal of our lives. God made us out of love and God is going to hold us in love through this life and into the next. Living the life of a saint is not about living a restricted, cautious, controlled life. It is about being fully alive; it is about drinking every bit of life to its last drop; it is about living a life of love. So on my mantel, next to my statue of St. Joseph, is a framed parchment with the following words which have become the mission statement for my life:

"Only one life that soon is past;
only what's done with love will last."

8

$\mathscr{B}$lessings For the Home

Prayer Service for the Burial of a St. Joseph Statue

Choose an attractive statue of St. Joseph that you will want to honor in your new home after the sale of your house.

Gather family and friends with you or ask them to pray with you on the day and hour that you bury the statue. Ask them to pray for all your needs concerning your home-making: that you sell the house, that the buyer will find it a good place to make a home, that your move be a time of new opportunities, that this transition in your life will be blessed with God's guidance, and other needs.

Dig a hole in a part of your property that is significant to you. The location doesn't matter. Bury the statue upside down, a humorous gesture indicating that the burial is a temporary state, soon to be set aright as you honor the statue in your new home.

A reading from the Gospel according to Luke:

When [Jesus'] parents saw him they were astonished; and his mother said to him, "Child, why have you treated us like this? Look, your father and I have been searching for you in great anxiety." He said to them, "Why were you searching for me? Did you not know that I must be in my Father's house?" But they did not understand what he said to them. Then he went down with them and came to Nazareth, and was obedient to them. His mother treasured all these things in her heart. And Jesus increased in wisdom and in years, and in divine and human favor (Luke 2:48-52).

A reading from the Gospel according to Matthew:

Everyone then who hears these words of mine and acts on them will be like a wise man who built his house on rock. The rain fell, the floods came, and the winds blew and beat on that house, but it did not fall, because it had been founded on rock. And everyone who hears these words of mine and does not act on them will be like a foolish man who built his house on sand. The rain fell, and the floods came, and the winds blew and beat against that house, and it fell—and great was its fall! (Matthew 7:24-27).

A Litany in Honor of St. Joseph:

Joseph, you are a son of Abraham, a member of the noble people of Israel.
All: St. Joseph, pray for us.

Joseph, you are a son of David, inheriting the royal promises of King David for your people.
All: St. Joseph, pray for us.

Joseph, you took Mary to be your wife and cared for her with the love of a husband.
All: St. Joseph, pray for us.

Joseph, you honored the vocation of marriage and family life.
All: St. Joseph, pray for us.

Joseph, you are the earthly father of the Son of God.
All: St. Joseph, pray for us.

Joseph, you are the guardian and protector of your family.
All: St. Joseph, pray for us.

Joseph, you built a house in Nazareth and provided a home for your family.
All: St. Joseph, pray for us.

Joseph, you moved your family from place to place, trusting in God's protection.
All: St. Joseph, pray for us.

Joseph, you were known as the carpenter, striving for excellence in all your work.
All: St. Joseph, pray for us.

Joseph, you are a model of patience, prudence, and justice.
All: St. Joseph, pray for us.

Let us pray:

Blessed are you, God of all creation. In your great love for all people, you have made Joseph of

Nazareth a humble instrument of your great plan to bring salvation to the world through Jesus, your Son. As husband, father, carpenter, and home-builder, Joseph knows our concerns as we seek to sell this house and create a new home. We ask that you hear his prayers for us and for all people experiencing moves and transitions.

Bless this house so that it may be a secure shelter for those who will be its new owners. May those who will live here find safety, prosperity, and tranquility within its walls. Help us to honor the life of Joseph and imitate the trusting faith he had in you and the devotion he showed to those he loved. Amen.

Concluding Blessing

"The Lord bless us and keep us; the Lord let his face shine upon us and be gracious to us; the Lord look upon us kindly and give us peace."

Prayer Service for Blessing a Home

This blessing may take place after moving into a new home and as an annual rededication. Family and friends may be invited to help you pray the home blessing.

A candle or cross may be carried to each room during the prayer, or a candle may be lit in each room as it is blessed.

Place the unearthed statue of St. Joseph in a place of honor in your new home. Include other religious symbols in the honored space, such as candles, flowers, a cross, a Bible, or other sacred images. Gather near the statue of Joseph as you begin.

Peace to this house and to all who live here.

A reading from Paul's letter to the Romans:

Let love be genuine; hate what is evil, hold fast to what is good; love one another with mutual affection; outdo one another in showing honor. Do not lag in zeal, be ardent in spirit, serve the Lord. Rejoice in hope, be patient in suffering, persevere in prayer. Contribute to the needs of the saints; extend hospitality to strangers. Bless those who persecute you; bless and do not curse them. Rejoice with those who rejoice, weep with those who weep. Live in harmony with one another; do not be haughty, but associate with the lowly; do not claim to be wiser than you are. Do not repay anyone evil for evil, but take thought for what is noble in the sight of all. If it is possible, so far as it depends on you, live peaceably with all (Romans 12:9-18).

Let Us Pray:

Eternal and loving God, whose home is in heaven and on earth, come with your blessings upon this house which has become our home. Transform this house into a sacred dwelling, filled with your presence. Protect this home from evil, bitterness, sickness, storm, or destruction. May we imitate the family life of Jesus, Mary, and Joseph, so that this home will be filled with joyful peace.

We thank you for the divine favors we have received through the prayers of St. Joseph. As he created a home for Jesus and Mary, through his work, faithfulness, and dedication to you, we invoke his continued prayers upon our home as we seek to live under his inspiration. We ask this prayer through Jesus, our Lord. Amen.

At the doorway:

Lord God, you commanded the people of Israel to write the commandment to love on the doorposts of their homes. May all our coming and going, our hellos and our goodbyes, be done in a spirit of love. Give us a spirit of hospitality to welcome visitors with honor and kindness and not turn away the person in need. May we recognize the spirit of Jesus in each person who comes to this door.

In the living room or family room:

God of life, this room is our place of renewal and refreshment. Bless all of our activities here: our conversation and entertainment, our work and our prayer. May each person who enjoys this room be filled with your peace. May the gifts of family and friendship grow and flourish in this place, giving joy to all who share it.

In the kitchen:

Abundant God, you give us our daily bread, supplying food and drink in abundance to meet our bodily needs. Bless the hands that work in this kitchen to prepare your gift of food, and make us grateful for the gifts from your bounty. Bless the pots and pans, and the herbs and spices. May the bitter seasonings of anger and resentment never spoil the meals prepared here.

In the dining room:

Gracious God, your word describes eternal life as a joyful feast in your kingdom. May all who share meals at this table be nourished in body, mind, and spirit. Bless the family and the friendships that grow and deepen around this table. May we always be grateful for your gifts to us and reach out to those who search for food and love.

In a bathroom:

Lord God, you have given us our bodies as temples of your Holy Spirit. Help us to care for our bodies and to honor them as your gift. Bless our lives with health and healing. Thank you for cleansing and refreshing waters and for the comforts that relieve the anxiety of each day.

In the bedroom:

Lord of life and love, bless this bedroom where we spend many hours of each day. Though we are not aware of your gifts in our sleeping, you bless us and sustain our lives even in rest. Help us to be grateful for your nightly protection and for the gift of dreams through which we can discover our hidden depths. Bless us each night with your gifts of affection and forgiveness, and bless us each morning with your refreshment.

In a child's room:

God of new life, bless this room which is a holy space for play, rest, study, and creativity. Embrace my child with your unfailing love and your constant care. May the conversations, music, and laughter that fill this room always give praise to you. Protect my child from all danger and harm, and give my child the gifts of happiness, trust, and confidence.

In the workroom or office:

Creator God, all our daily work is a sharing in your creating power. Bless this place to be used for work at home. Help us to be skillful and productive in the many projects and tasks we undertake. You made human work a holy task through the earthly labor of Jesus, your Son. Bless us with a spirit of joy and accomplishment in all the work that is completed here. May the work of our lives always give you honor.

In the yard, garden, patio, or deck:

God of all the world, you've given us the beauty of the open air which expands the boundaries of our home into the world of nature. Bless this outdoor space with the gift of your peace and tranquility. Help us make this a place of relaxation, recreation, and hospitality. May the birds, trees, grass, and flowers remind us not to worry about tomorrow, for you know our every need.

Concluding Blessing

"The Lord bless us and keep us; the Lord let his face shine upon us and be gracious to us; the Lord look upon us kindly and give us peace."

A Spouse's Prayer

God of Love, you made Joseph a faithful spouse through the blessings of marriage. He chose Mary, cherished her, protected her, and provided a home for her. Through the prayers of Joseph, help me to be a good and faithful spouse to the one I have chosen. Give me the grace to continually honor my spouse with devotion and care. May the struggles and routine of life never dilute our love, nor the hardships and worries of life compromise our dedication to each other.

Help me to take the time to listen to my spouse and to speak words that I have chosen with care. When I fail, give me the courage to ask for forgiveness; when I am wronged, give me the grace to forgive. May I praise and thank you always for the gift of my spouse and for the gift of our love.

St. Joseph, pray for me and the one I love. Amen.

A Parent's Prayer

God of all families, you made Joseph the earthly father of your Son, Jesus. He honored his son in Mary's womb, protected his infant son from danger, taught his growing child the ways of faith, trained him to work, and raised him to be a man. Like Joseph, I worry about providing for my children, about their safety, about their education, about their self-confidence.

Through the prayers of Joseph, help me to be a good parent and give me the wisdom to speak and act in love. I want to be a model, a comforter, a guide, and a companion along the way of life for my children. Help me to praise and encourage at least as much as I correct and discipline. When I fail them, help me to admit my wrong and seek forgiveness. Let me always realize that my children are a precious treasure loaned to me from you. Guide me as I try to help my children become who you created them to be.

St. Joseph, pray for me and surround my children with your fatherly care. Amen.

A Prayer for Daily Work

God of all creation, through our daily work you have made us stewards of the earth and co-creators with you. As a skilled carpenter, Joseph worked in Nazareth and taught Jesus the dignity of human work and the nobility of manual labor. Through the example of Joseph, teach me to work productively, skillfully, and honestly.

As I go about my work this day, help me to value the things I do, whether they be big projects or tiring, trivial tasks. Enable me to handle the stresses of my work and to trust in your guiding presence. Show me that my workaday living is my road to holiness. May my Sunday worship blend into my weekday labor so that all that I do each day may give you praise.

St. Joseph the Worker, pray for me and be my example in everyday work. Amen.